SpringerBriefs in Criminology

Policing

Series Editor

M. R. Haberfeld
City University of New York
John Jay College of Criminal Justice
New York, NY, USA

SpringerBriefs in Criminology present concise summaries of cutting edge research across the fields of Criminology and Criminal Justice. It publishes small but impactful volumes of between 50-125 pages, with a clearly defined focus. The series covers a broad range of Criminology research from experimental design and methods, to brief reports and regional studies, to policy-related applications.

The scope of the series spans the whole field of Criminology and Criminal Justice, with an aim to be on the leading edge and continue to advance research. The series will be international and cross-disciplinary, including a broad array of topics, including juvenile delinquency, policing, crime prevention, terrorism research, crime and place, quantitative methods, experimental research in criminology, research design and analysis, forensic science, crime prevention, victimology, criminal justice systems, psychology of law, and explanations for criminal behavior.

SpringerBriefs in Criminology will be of interest to a broad range of researchers and practitioners working in Criminology and Criminal Justice Research and in related academic fields such as Sociology, Psychology, Public Health, Economics and Political Science.

More information about this series at http://www.springer.com/series/11179

Mohsen Alizadeh

Police Policy Shifts After 9/11

From Community Policing to Homeland Security: A New York Case Study

Mohsen Alizadeh
Danbury, CT, USA

ISSN 2192-8533   ISSN 2192-8541   (electronic)
SpringerBriefs in Criminology
ISSN 2194-6213   ISSN 2194-6221   (electronic)
SpringerBriefs in Policing
ISBN 978-3-030-32122-2   ISBN 978-3-030-32123-9   (eBook)
https://doi.org/10.1007/978-3-030-32123-9

© The Author(s), under exclusive license to Springer Nature Switzerland AG 2020
This work is subject to copyright. All rights are solely and exclusively licensed by the Publisher, whether the whole or part of the material is concerned, specifically the rights of translation, reprinting, reuse of illustrations, recitation, broadcasting, reproduction on microfilms or in any other physical way, and transmission or information storage and retrieval, electronic adaptation, computer software, or by similar or dissimilar methodology now known or hereafter developed.
The use of general descriptive names, registered names, trademarks, service marks, etc. in this publication does not imply, even in the absence of a specific statement, that such names are exempt from the relevant protective laws and regulations and therefore free for general use.
The publisher, the authors, and the editors are safe to assume that the advice and information in this book are believed to be true and accurate at the date of publication. Neither the publisher nor the authors or the editors give a warranty, express or implied, with respect to the material contained herein or for any errors or omissions that may have been made. The publisher remains neutral with regard to jurisdictional claims in published maps and institutional affiliations.

This Springer imprint is published by the registered company Springer Nature Switzerland AG
The registered company address is: Gewerbestrasse 11, 6330 Cham, Switzerland

Contents

1 Introduction and Theoretical Framework 1
   Theoretical Framework 2
      Focusing Events Theory 2
      Moral Panic Theory 4
   The Link Between the Theoretical Framework and Examined
   Variables 5
   References 5

2 Research on Community Policing and Homeland Security 7
   Previous Research 7
   Community Policing National Survey in 2002 Compared
   to the Last Two Surveys 8
   Research on Funding Community Policing 9
   Research on Implementation of Community Policing 10
   The Impact of September 11, 2001 11
   Homeland Security and Community Policing 12
   Shortcomings of Prior Research 13
   References 14

3 Methodology 15
   The Purpose of This Research 15
      Research Questions 16
      Sample 17
      Data Collection 18
   Intervening Variables 20
      Importance of Intervening Variables 21
      Data Aggregation 21
      New York City's Data and Data Aggregation 21
   Research Design and Data Analysis 23
   References 25

4	**Results**	27
	NYC Community Policing Results	27
	NYC General Policing Results	30
	NYC Homeland Security Results	33
	NYC Policing From 2012 To 2019	36
	Findings Summary	37
	References	38
5	**Summary**	39
	Discussion	39
	Study's Findings and Focusing Events Theory	39
	Study's Findings and Moral Panic Theory	40
	Study's Findings and Other Literatures	40
	Limitations	41
	Potential Contribution and Policy Implication	42
	References	43

Appendix 45

Index 47

About the Author

Professor Alizadeh holds a Ph.D. in Criminal Justice, Master of Philosophy from the City University of New York (Graduate Center), Master's Degree in Criminal Justice from John Jay College of Criminal Justice, Master's Degree in Criminal Law and Criminology from Islamic Azad University Central Tehran Branch, and Bachelor's Degree of Law from Islamic Azad University Rafsanjan Branch.

He joined the Division of Justice and Law Administration at Western Connecticut State University in 2016 with 11 years of teaching experience. Prior to joining Western Connecticut State University, he was teaching at the State University of New York, Montclair State University of New Jersey, and John Jay College of Criminal Justice.

His research focus on policing systems, theory testing in public policy, and comparative criminal justice systems. He is also a book editor for International Police Executive Symposium (IPES).

Chapter 1
Introduction and Theoretical Framework

The purpose of this research is to examine the impact of the September 11 terrorist attack on funded research in the fields of Community Policing, General Policing, and Homeland Security in terms of federal grants in New York City (NYC). After the professional model of policing ended, community policing claimed to be an effective model in the United States of America.

However, in the aftermath of September 11, Homeland Security introduced new organizational policies to the U.S. criminal justice system, which affected community policing (CP). This research seeks to identify the impact of such policies on research grant allocation for community policing research. Although some scholars believe that federal assistance to community policing has evaporated (Lee 2010), this claim was not supported with empirical research.

The current research intends to use the *pre-experimental design (before-and-after design)* method to examine the U.S. Census database to search for the grants awarded to community policing prior to and after the September 11 event in New York City in order to discover if there have been any negative or positive effects on community policing grants post September 11. Specifically, this research aims to examine federal grant opportunities as an indication of *shift in police policy*.

The Violent Crime Control Act of 1994 authorized billions of dollars from 1995 to 2000 in the form of grants allocated to local police departments to hire more officers and expand community-policing programs. It was this Act that created the office of Community Oriented Policing Services (COPS), which supplemented several types of funding including Making Hiring Officer Redeployment Effective (MORE) funds and other innovative grants (Worrall and Kovandzic 2007). Researchers have been evaluating COPS money in order to assess its outcome (Zhao et al. 2011; Worrall and Kovandzic 2007).

Research findings are not consistent. For instance, some findings show positive relationships between COPS hiring grants and all four types of police arrests (Zhao et al. 2011). However, other researchers contend that their data shows COPS grants had little to no effect on crime (Worrall and Kovandzic 2007). Conflicting results

---

© The Author(s), under exclusive license to Springer Nature Switzerland AG 2020
M. Alizadeh, *Police Policy Shifts After 9/11*, SpringerBriefs in Criminology,
https://doi.org/10.1007/978-3-030-32123-9_1

like these make it unclear whether or not the COPS grants have led to the reduction of crimes. Therefore, it is important to have the trends of the grant's money allocated to COPS programs to develop new policies or modify existing programs. While researchers were evaluating the outcomes of COPS programs, the September 11 attacks occurred. This catastrophic event resulted in some inevitable changes to the American policing system. The changes were introduced without sufficient scholarly research.

In the aftermath of the September 11 attacks, Homeland Security (HS) was established. Soon after its establishment, HS recognized the value of local police agencies and started to lend them financial support. For instance, $400 million was allocated as terrorism prevention grants to local agencies. Police departments became "intelligence gatherers" as well as first respondents (Friedmann and Cannon 2007). However, this new practice of policing might not be fully comparable to the philosophy of community policing. Furthermore, the allocation of funds has been changed from community policing to security concerns under HS. For instance, in the 1990s, the Office of Community Oriented Policing Service (COPS) spent about one billion dollars each year on local agencies for hiring purposes, but this amount was reduced to less than $200 million for the fiscal year of 2003. Furthermore, the entire COPS funding for the year 2004 was reduced from $738 million to $164 million. The funds radically shifted from community policing to HS practice (De Simone 2003; Geraghty 2003).

Under the rising influence of HS, community-policing programs were the recipients of an "unprecedented level" of federal grants (Lee 2010). The former focus on policing was challenged by HS. Consequently, after the 9/11 attacks, the direction of community policing funds shifted toward HS, which is an indication of a major policy modification. Such a shift in grant allocation will be the focus of the current study.

Theoretical Framework

Focusing Events Theory

After the occurrence of any catastrophic event, society's reaction is to change current policies to prevent similar incidents from occurring in the future. The policy changes after the occurrence of such events are well known to scholars. Events can change policies and shift funds in different directions. Kingdon believes that some vivid events that have negative impacts on society are also able to cause the general public as well as public officials to pay more attention to the root cause of those events (Kingdon 1984). Scholars also mention the importance of events that seize public attention as potential causes of policy change (Cobb and Elder 1983; Light 1999; & Walker 1977). These catalytic events are known as *focusing events* (Birkland 1998). For instance, in 1993 a natural gas pipeline exploded near an apartment building in Edison, N.J (Pena 1994).

Theoretical Framework

This accident drove state officials to enact obligatory regulations for contractors to notify neighborhoods prior to digging close to pipelines (Birkland 1997). Some *focusing events* are capable of changing and shifting governments' funding in other directions and instigating the development of new policies as well. For instance, the energy challenges after the Fukushima incident provoked some countries to change their policies on nuclear reactors. Chinese officials announced that they had ceased approving the construction of any new nuclear plants in the country (Popescu and Leca 2012). Safety review and stress tests took place in nearly all countries using nuclear plants. In particular, Germany decided to shut down all of the reactors that had been in operation prior to 1980 and also announced that all others would be closed by 2022 (Popescu and Leca 2012). Furthermore, Italy had a referendum in June 2011 to close all nuclear programs permanently (Popescu and Leca 2012). Therefore, the Fukushima incident can be used as an example of an event that results in drastic public policy changes at an international level.

Birkland claims that three *focusing events* in the aviation history of the U.S. were the cause of major policy changes:

1. Pan Am flight 103 bombing over Lockerbie, Scotland, which killed all the passengers as well as eleven people on the ground. This focusing event resulted in enacting the Aviation Security Improvement Act of 1990, which required giving greater attention to explosive detection and instigated organizational changes in the Department of State and Federal Aviation Administration (FAA) regarding intelligence information (Birkland 2004);
2. The explosion of TWA flight 800 over the Atlantic Ocean near Long Island, New York. This incident occurred because of an overheated empty fuel tank with fuel fumes. When a spark was introduced to the tank from fuel level devices, both the fuel tank and the airplane exploded. This dramatic event resulted in the Federal Aviation Authorization Act of 1996. The Act mandated the profiling of passengers by the FAA; the usage of explosive detection; and the implementation of the baggage-matching system (Birkland 2004);
3. Finally, but of no less importance, is the hijacking of planes for the September 11 attacks. This event caused major changes to take place in aviation security policies throughout the Aviation and Transportation Security Act (Birkland 2004). Evidence of such a change in aviation policy clearly establishes September 11 as a focusing event. There is an equally likelihood of its being a focusing event with respect to changes in community policing.

Using the *focusing events* theory, one might conclude that the aviation policy modification was not the sole effect of September 11. The incident also produced other policy changes. When the World Trade Center and the Pentagon were attacked, the establishment of the department of Homeland Security as the prime agency to fight and prevent similar incidents became the priority of the Federal Government, which once again pushed the policing system in another direction. The direction of funds was shifted from community policing to Homeland Security as well. The Homeland Security office identified four goals for its existence: (a) prevention of terrorist attacks; (b) protection of the key resources and critical infrastructure of the

U.S.; (c) responding to incidents that have already occurred as well as recovering from them; and (d) continuing to strengthen the foundation of Homeland Security to ensure long term success (Kappeler and Gaines 2011). This was a major policy change resulting from the *focusing event* of September 11.

If the theory is correct, one can therefore conclude that September 11 changed the policing direction to one different from what it was previously because the theory suggests that incidents like this are capable of altering public policy as well as shifting the direction of funds. Using this theory, one can predict not only that the event changed the format of policing from community policing to Homeland Security, but also that it shifted funds from community policing to Homeland Security. This prediction can be used as an answer to the research questions of the study and explain why the observed variables exist. The theory also can provide explanations for interpretation of the results.

Moral Panic Theory

Moral panic theory concerns situations where a society encounters acts of malevolence by malefactors and exaggerates the degree of harm inflicted by them or even imagines additional harm. Communities' reactions to these threats or harms are disproportionate to the actual threats. Sociologists call this *"moral panic"* and wrongdoers are named *folk devils* (Good and Ben-Yehuda 2009).

Any incident might activate *moral panic*. In 1949, when the mutilated body of a young girl was found in Los Angeles, mass media paid special attention to a number of similar past crimes. When Fred Stroble was arrested as the first suspect, the Los Angeles District Attorney extracted a confession from the defendant, who also agreed to meet with reporters and repeat his confession.

Following such incidents, many states passed *sexual psychopath laws*. Sutherland believes the enacting of these laws was associated with the manipulation of public demands by the press and the influence of psychiatrists on the process of legislation (Sutherland 1950).

Moral panic needs a variety of actors to fully evolve. Cohen (1972) believes that mass media, the public opinion, police, social activists, politicians and legislators are primary actors in the drama of moral panic. He pays special attention to the press as the most important actor, because the media can easily ignite the attention of both politicians and the public. Cohen also believes that mass media is capable of exaggerating incidents, makings false stories, and overstressing the seriousness of any situation. A *folk devil* is a suitable enemy for effecting moral panic because it represents evil. Therefore, moral panic divides society into "them /devils" and "us/ law abiding citizens" (Cohen 1972). Goode and Ben-Yehuda recognized five basic elements of moral panic: *(a) concern or fear; (b) hostility toward the folk devil; (c) some consensus about the nature of the threat; (d) a disproportion between the concern and the threat; (e) a certain degree of volatility of the concern* (Good and Ben-Yehuda 2009, p. 49). They also add that moral panic expresses itself in different ways: public opinion, media, social movement with accompanying political activities and law enforcement.

The moral panic theory of Ben-Yehuda and Goode will be used to examine the implications of post-September 11 on federal grants allocation and the possible change in funding venues.

The Link Between the Theoretical Framework and Examined Variables

Focusing events and moral panic are two main theories that provide theoretical contexts for the study. These theories are being used to have a potentially better understanding of the effects of the September 11 attacks (independent variable) on community policing funds (dependent variable), while enabling the researcher an opportunity to further examine and confront the theories.

1. Focusing event theory: if the theory is correct, one can therefore conclude that September 11 changed the policing direction to one different from what it was previously because the theory suggests that incidents like this are capable of altering public policy as well as shifting the direction of funds. Using this theory, one can predict not only the event changed the format of policing from community policing to Homeland Security, but also that it shifted funds from community policing to Homeland Security. This prediction can be used as an answer to research questions of the study to explain why the observed variables exist. It can also enable an interpretation of the results.
2. Moral panic theory: *folk devils* (i.e., sexual psychopaths, hijackers, etc.) are the most suitable for enabling the media to generate fear, which consequently results in the demand for change by the general public. Politicians have made those changes, for instance, by transforming the community policing system into Homeland Security. This has resulted in cutting or discontinuing community policing funds. This will be the probable answer to the research questions of this study and will also enable interpreting the outcome of the research with the help of theoretical frameworks.

References

Birkland, T. (1997). *After disaster: Agenda setting, public policy, and focusing events*. Washington, DC: Georgetown University Press.
Birkland, T. (1998). Focusing events, mobilization and agenda setting. *Journal of Public Policy*, 18(1), 53–74. Cambridge, UK: Cambridge University.
Birkland, T. (2004). Learning and policy improvement after disaster: The case of aviation security. *American Behavioral Scientist, 48*, 341–364. https://doi.org/10.1177/0002764204268990.
Cobb, R., & Elder, C. (1983). *Participation in American politics: The dynamics of agenda-building* (2nd ed.). Baltimore: Johns Hopkins University Press.

Cohen, S. (1972). *Folk devils and moral panics*. London: MacGibbon & Kee Ltd.

De Simone, D. C. (2003, April). Federal budget a mixed bag for state and local governments. *Government Finance Review, 19*(2), 66–69.

Friedmann, R., & Cannon, W. (2007). Homeland security and community policing: Competing or complementing public safety policies. *Journal of Homeland Security and Emergency Management, 4*(4).

Geraghty, J. (2003, April 9). Democratic study indicates police strain under homeland securities duties. States News Service, p. 1008099u1552.

Good, E., & Ben-Yehuda, N. (2009). *Moral panics: The social construction of deviance* (2nd ed.). West Sussex: Blackwell Publishing.

Kappeler, V., & Gaines, L. (2011). *Community policing: A contemporary perspective* (6th ed.). Waltham: Anderson Publishing.

Kingdon, J. (1984). *Agendas, alternatives, and public policies*. Boston: Little Brown, and Company.

Lee, V. J. (2010). *Community policing in an age of homeland security*. Police Quarterly: SAGE Publications.

Light, P. (1999). *The president's agenda: Domestic policy choice from Kennedy to Clinton* (3rd ed.). Baltimore: The John Hopkins University Press.

Pena, R. (1994, March). *Huge gas pipeline explosion rocks*. Northeast New Jersey: The New York Times.

Popescu, E., & Leca, A. (2012). The energy challenges after Fukushima. *U.P.B. Scientific Bulletin Series C, 74*(3).

Sutherland, E. (1950, September). The sexual psychopath law. *American Journal of Sociology, LVI*, 142–148.

Walker, J. (1977,. October)). Setting the agenda in the U.S. Senate: A theory of problem selection. *British Journal of Political Science, 7*(4), 423–445.

Worrall, J. L., & Kovandzic. (2007). Cops grants and crime revisited. *Criminology, 45*, 159–190. https://doi.org/10.1111/j.1745-9125.2007.00075.x.

Zhao, J., Zhang, Y., & Thurman, Q. (2011, June). Can additional resources lead to higher levels of productivity (arrests) in police agencies? *Criminal Justice Review, 36*(2), 165–182.

Chapter 2
Research on Community Policing and Homeland Security

Previous Research

By reviewing the research related to community policing (CP), one can examine whether the concept of CP has been implemented by those agencies that adopted it. As Goldstein (1993) notes, community policing has been widely used without paying attention to its substance. Furthermore, politicians use its label to create a popular image (Goldstein 1993). Therefore, it is imperative to examine the real extent of CP. To do this, two different national surveys were conducted in 1992 and 1997 regarding community policing. Using the Likert scale, the police departments in both surveys were asked to agree or disagree with the following comment: *"It is not clear what community policing means in practical terms."* In 1992, 47% of departments agreed or strongly agreed with the sentence. Those who agreed with the same sentence in 1997 amounted to 31%, indicating police departments have developed their understanding of community policing over time. Almost 50% of police departments did not have a clear understanding of community policing in practice in 1992. However, only 30% of police departments had the same problem in 1997. This study was conducted by the Police Foundation, which was funded by the Department of Justice. About 2337 police departments participated in the study. The second survey (1997) was conducted by the Opinion Research Corporation Company (ORC) and the Police Executive Research Forum (PERF) and received responses from 1637 different police departments (Fridell 2004). The author also discusses the following findings of these two surveys:

- *We have not considered adopting a* community policing *approach.* 28% of agencies in 1992 agreed with the above comment while only 5% of departments agreed with it in 1997, indicating that within 5 years of adopting it, community policing had 23% growth.
- *We considered adopting a* community policing *approach but rejected the idea because it was not appropriate for the agency.* 3% of police departments indicated

---

© The Author(s), under exclusive license to Springer Nature Switzerland AG 2020
M. Alizadeh, *Police Policy Shifts After 9/11*, SpringerBriefs in Criminology,
https://doi.org/10.1007/978-3-030-32123-9_2

they agree with this sentence in 1992 while only 2% of them agreed with the same sentence 5 years later.

- *We considered a* community policing *approach and liked the idea but it is not practical here at this time.* 18% of agencies agreed with this idea in 1992 while only 8% of them agreed with it in 1997.
- *We are now in the process of planning or implementing a community policing approach.* 31% said yes to this concept in 1992 and another 21% adopted it 5 years later.
- *We have implemented community policing.* 20% of agencies agreed with this concept in 1992 while the result of the 1997 survey shows that 58% of departments implemented CP.

These results show the significant changes over only 5 years in the practice of community policing (Fridell 2004). Therefore, one can conclude that the community-policing philosophy experienced a positive growth from 1992 to 1997, and had been implemented widely in the U.S.

In another article, using data from Virginia police chiefs, Chappell and Gibson (2009) tried to examine the chiefs' attitudes at the time of Homeland Security. Their results showed not only that many police chiefs believed, because of Homeland Security, the emphasis on community policing had been reduced, but also that they viewed HS and CP as "*complimentary strategies*". Researchers also proved that department chiefs with the full implication of community policing are less likely to accept reducing the role of CP. Their findings also show that chiefs from departments with fewer than 5000 citizens also do not see community policing waning. It is interesting to note that the authors' findings indicate that chiefs with at least 4 years of college are less likely to accept that the role of community policing has been reduced after the Homeland Security era. In fact, they view these two types of policing as complementary (Chappell and Gibson 2009).

However, none of the above surveys were associated with examining the budgets and grants that were devoted to community policing. If police agencies have received federal funds to implement the practice of community policing, it would be impossible to use those grants for any other purposes.

Therefore, expansion of the practice might be due to available funds. Previous researches have not examined the association of federal grants with the expansion of the community policing practice. This requires new research to fill the existing gap. In contrast, this research aims to inspect the grant funds of each year for community policing to see if such granted money had been increased or decreased following the events of September 11.

Community Policing National Survey in 2002 Compared to the Last Two Surveys

The Police Executive Research Forum (PERF) decided to modify the survey that was used for the aforementioned two studies in order to collect additional information and to track any change in the practice of community policing. To do so, PERF targeted only those agencies that had responded to the first two surveys and reported that they had practiced community policing. 282 agencies were identified. Among them, 240 responded to the new survey (Fridell 2004). 90% of police agencies in all three surveys reported that community policing: (1) improved cooperation between citizens and police; (2) increased citizen involvement; (3) increased information exchanged between citizens and police; (4) improved citizens' attitudes toward police; and (5) it reduced citizens' fear of crime. Fridell also mentions that between 1992 and 2002, survey agencies reported that the community policing practice resulted in: (1) less physical conflict between police and citizens; (2) job satisfaction of officers along with an increase in the voluntary activities of citizens; and (3) a decrease in violent and property crimes (Fridell 2004). However, the 2002 survey did not include an examination of grant money deriving from the Federal Government to community policing to have a more comprehensive view. Agencies that expanded the practice of community policing might have done so because of the grant money and vice versa. This research will shed light in that area to provide a more comprehensive view.

Research on Funding Community Policing

Zhao et al. (2002) studied the effect of community policing grants on violent and property crimes from 1995 to 1999. Their analysis shows COPS hiring and innovative grant programs significantly reduced the crime rates in cities with populations of 10,000 and more. Researchers also showed that adding one-dollar for innovative grants for each resident of cities with populations of 10,000 and more will result in a 12.93% decrease in violent crimes and also a reduction in property crimes by 45.53% per 100,000 residents. Furthermore, their findings proved community policing grants for cities with populations of 10,000 and less have no negative impact (Zhao et al. 2002). According to the authors, *"up to the year of 2002 there was no comprehensive national study of the overall effects of COPS grants (specially designed to support this community policing efforts) on crime in the United States"* (Zhao et al. 2002, p. 12).

Their research was the first that tried to establish a link between the dollar amounts (grant) devoted to community policing and decreasing crimes. However, the study did not compare and contrast each year's grant to other years to see if there were any differences.

Under the policy recommendations researchers suggested that federal grants should be made directly to police departments to promote innovations and the hiring of more officers to reduce property and violent crime rates (Zhao et al. 2002). However, it is not clear whether the recommended policy has been implemented. In fact, the current research aims to clarify this issue and ascertain as to whether the recommended policy has been implemented.

Evans and Owens (2007) focused on money from grants that were received from Community Oriented Policing Service (COPS) to increase the size of police forces to see if this increase resulted in lower crime rates. They noticed the crime rate reduction of four out of eight index crimes (auto theft, burglary, robbery, and aggravated assault) for those areas that received COPS money to hire more officers. The researchers also found agencies that used COPS grants to increase police technology also resulted in drops in the aforementioned four crime categories as well as in larcenies (Evans and Owens 2007).

In a different study, Zhao et al. (2011) also found that there is a positive relationship between COPS hiring grants and all types of police arrests. Additionally, they claimed not only that the hiring grant was a significant predictor of arrests, but also that more manpower is also related to police arrests (Zhao et al. 2011).

However, not only are the literature findings not consistent, but in some instances, they are potentially confusing. Worrall and Kovandzic (2007) claim that all of the aforementioned findings are not consistent with the results of their study. They claim that some eight billion of taxpayers' money to be spent by COPS is not connected to crime reduction. Since their results show that "COPS spending had little to no effect on crime" (Worrall and Kovandzic 2007, p.159), they believe allocating federal money for local police is not the best policy for reducing crime.

Therefore, there are two different scenarios to consider: (a) if COPS money resulted in lower crime rates, then we know that adding more money to community policing will translate to the reduction of crime rates; and (b) if the COPS money is not correlated to crime reduction, then all of the granted federal money to COPS program was wasted, and it is imperative to have policy change considerations. For both scenarios, we do not know how much money was devoted to community policing prior to and after September 11. Due to the lack of research, it is also unknown whether the event of September 11 had a positive or negative impact on grant money allocated for community policing. Consequently, further study is needed to examine the allocation of grants to community policing, which is the main goal of this current study.

Research on Implementation of Community Policing

The Bureau of Justice Assistance Support established Innovative Neighborhood Oriented Policing (INOP) programs in eight cities in 1990 to reduce drug problems. Each site received between $100,000 and $200,000 in the first year of the program. INOP chose both small and big cities to implement CP and evaluated the results. Hayward, CA, Houston, TX, New York, NY, Norfolk, VA, Portland, OR, Prince George County, MD, and Tempe, Arizona were chosen for the study. These projects were evaluated by NIJ and the Vera Institute of Justice (Sadd and Grinc 1996). The major finding of these studies was that it was difficult for officers in all of the above-mentioned districts to adopt new behavioral role as Community Policing Officers. Involving citizens was also a challenge for the program. Despite the fact that projects were associated with training, officers' resistance was the major problem when implementing community policing. Both trained and non-trained officers envisioned community outreach and new relationships between police and society, but only some of them mention problem solving as a major element of community policing. Most of them envisioned real police work as involving crime related issues. Because of the fact that INOP was a new experience of community policing for most of the agencies, the projects started as separate new units, which also led to conflicts between the traditional practice of policing and community policing. The study also found that most people believe that the police-public relationship has been improved, but the program had little effect on reducing drug problems (Sadd and Grinc 1996). However, authors suggest that community policing required more resources for proper implementation and also transitions from traditional policing to community policing. Whether this policy recommendation has been implemented is not clear. There is no comprehensive research following federal grants to see what percentage of the federal rewards was spent on community policing each year. Current research is examining this issue to see if the above recommendation has been implemented.

There is a partnership between the Bureau of Justice Statistics and the office of Community Oriented Policing Service. Hickman and Reaves (2001) collected both of these institutions' related data in 1997 and 1999. Their data shows that 34% of agencies used community policing in 1997, while 64% of agencies used community policing practices in 1999 (almost double the amount). The research also indicates that the number of community policing officers were 21,000 in 1997 compared to 113,000 in 1999, which means more than a fivefold increase in about 2 years (Hickman and Reaves 2001). This research shows the practice of community policing has increased up to 1997. However, this study had been conducted prior to September 11. It is unclear whether the community policing practice was expanded after the event. The event might have affected community policing positively or negatively. Thus far, no study has been done to determine the effects. The current proposal intends to measure the aforementioned impacts following the federal grants money devoted to community policing to determine if September 11 had any correlation with the practice of community policing.

The Impact of September 11, 2001

Since the national survey of 2002 (mentioned in "Community Policing National Survey in 2002 Compared to the Last Two Surveys") was conducted after September 11, it seems appropriate to design some questions in this new survey to measure the impact of September 11 on community policing.

Police Executive Research Forum (PERF) also noted the need and asked the agencies the following questions:

> *"To what extent do you think the events of September 11, 2001 will impact your agency's community policing efforts?"* (Fridell 2004, p. 55).

Not surprisingly, 58% of agencies believed that the attack would affect their practice of community policing to *some extent*. Another 11% reported that the impact would be to *"a great extent"*, and about 1/3 of agencies believed that the event would not impact their practices at all. Therefore, the majority of the agencies (61%) reported that September 11 would have a negative impact on community policing. They assumed so because they believed officers have other priorities, since: (1) the moving of line officers from patrol to security assignments; (2) the need to fight against domestic terrorism might take time and resources away from community policing; (3) giving military assignment to the officers, thus creating many holes in schedules; and (4) a higher level of routine patrol would take away the number of officers that should be devoted to community policing (Fridell 2004).

There are some issues regarding the 2002 survey that should be addressed. First, agencies were asked: *What do you think about community policing after September 11?* It is obvious that researchers were trying to measure the agencies' perception toward community policing after the September 11 event. However, the real impact of the event might have been far from what agencies presumed it to be. To measure the real impacts, different studies should be conducted, including examining the budgets devoted to community policing each year, or reviewing the grant money that should have been spent on community policing. Such studies have yet to be conducted.

Second, the study was done in 2002, only 1 year after the September 11 event, whereas community policing practices have existed since 1960s. If one wants to examine the true impact of September 11, it is more appropriate to conduct a pre-experimental study to examine both long and short-term impacts.

Homeland Security and Community Policing

When the World Trade Center and the Pentagon were attacked, Homeland Security became the first priority of the Federal Government and once again pushed the policing system into another direction. Funds changed direction from community policing to Homeland Security as well. The Homeland Security office identified four goals for its existence: (a) Prevention of terrorist attacks; (b) Protecting Americans, key resources, and critical infrastructure; (c) responding to and recovering from incidents; and finally, (d) to continuing to strengthen the foundation of Homeland Security to ensure long-term success (Kappeler and Gaines 2011).

Immediately after the September 11 attack, police agencies at all levels shifted their focus to the old practice of policing to fortify the U.S. All domestic flights were canceled, international flights were diverted, and immigration officials and U.S. Customs prevented the flow of traffic across the borders. Furthermore, both political parties united to pass an antiterrorism Act, which resulted in passing the U.S.A. PATRIOT Act. In addition, following the event, the reorganization of federal law enforcement agencies took place, which created the Department of Homeland Security and Transportation Security Administration (Brown 2007).

Notably, those counterterrorism provisions violated the basic requirement of community policing. For instance, community policing tries to bridge the gap between the police and society by building trust between them, but the PATRIOT Act permits wiretapping phones, arresting people without warrants, etc. Not only are these policies contrary to community policing practice, but they also may not be compatible with the constitution.

Brown's conception of the effects of September 11 on community policing is:

> *In sum, the war on terrorism has taken a toll on the community policing movement. There has been an increase in aggressive security measures such as proactive patrols around national landmarks, an increase in technologically enhanced investigative tactics such as bugging homes, and a decrease in Federal funding for community policing efforts. However, there is little evidence to suggest that the decrease in support for community policing or the increased use of aggressive tactics and invasive technology will either reduce the threat of terrorism or be an effective means of controlling crime and disorder* (Brown 2007, p. 242).

Brown claimed that the Federal Government cut the amount of funds of community policing, but he had not evaluated the grants money allocated to both HS and CP to see whether community policing funds decreased. Therefore, there is a need to investigate this further.

Lee (2010) showed that the practice of CP and HS are in fact compatible. He also believes that his data proves that it is possible to have HS policing associated with community policing programs. This indicates that the Homeland Security approach is not necessarily at odds with community policing. Furthermore, Lee suggests that more data is needed to conduct further studies (Lee 2010) but such data has yet to be collected.

Shortcomings of Prior Research

Previously mentioned research projects show that in some extensions community policing was negatively affected by the events of September 11 (Friedmann and Cannon 2007; De Simone 2003; Geraghty 2003; Zhao et al. 2002). However, it is obvious that the full impact of September 11 on community policing is still unclear. Most of the prior mentioned research studies show only a snapshot of a single wave. These studies are known as *cross-sectional* studies, which have an essential problem. While the goal of conducting such studies is to explore causal processes over time, the inferences being made are only based on a single observation (Maxfiled and Babbie 2012). To have a better overview and assess the full impact of 9/11, a *pre-experimental design* is suggested in this study to enable the establishment of a causal relationship between the September 11 event and changes in community policing funding. There are a number of ways to measure the effects of September 11 on community policing. One way is to follow the federal grants on both community policing and public safety programs related to Homeland Security to measure the impacts over a period of many years rather than limiting it to 1 year. Reviewing the scholarly literature indicates that such a study has yet to be conducted. Accordingly, the purpose of this research is to examine federal funds granted to both community policing and HS from the date they were established. In addition, the research will investigate the allocation of money for these two institutions to find out how the events of September 11 affected the practice of community policing with the shifting of funds.

Prior studies (Fridell 2004) show the practice of community policing was associated with many positive issues. Some of them are as follows: better cooperation between police and people, increased citizen involvement, improvement of peoples' attitudes towards police, less conflict between citizens and police, etc.

However, such studies did not present a comprehensive view of the problem since they did not contain an examination of grant money derived from the Federal Government for community policing. Agencies that expanded the practice might have done so because of the grant money and vice versa.

References

Brown, B. (2007). Community policing in post-September 11 America: A comment on the concept of community-oriented counterterrorism. *Police Practice and Research, 8*, 239–251.

Chappell, A. T., & Gibson, S. A. (2009). Community policing and homeland security policing: Friend or foe? *Criminal Justice Policy Review, 20*(3), 326–343.

De Simone, D. C. (2003, April). Federal budget a mixed bag for state and local governments. *Government Finance Review, 19*(2), 66–69.

Evans, W. N., & Owens, E. G. (2007). COPS and crime. *Journal of Public Economics, 91*(1–2), 181–201.

Fridell, L. (2004). The results of three national surveys on community policing. In L. Fidel & M. Wyoff (Eds.), *Community policing, past, present and future* (pp. 39–58).. Police Executive Research Forum). Washington, DC: The Annie E. Casey Foundation.

Friedmann, R., & Cannon, W. (2007). Homeland security and community policing: Competing or complementing public safety policies. *Journal of Homeland Security and Emergency Management, 4*(4).

Geraghty, J. (2003, April 9). Democratic study indicates police strain under homeland securities duties. States News Service, p. 1008099u1552.

Goldstein, H. (1993). The new policing, confronting complexity. In *National institute of justice, research in brief*. Washington, DC: U.S. Department of Justice.

Hickman, M., & Reaves, B. (2001). Community policing in local police departments. Bureau of justice statistics, Special report.

Kappeler, V., & Gaines, L. (2011). *Community policing: A contemporary perspective* (6th ed.). Waltham: Anderson Publishing.

Lee, V. J. (2010). Community policing in an age of homeland security. Police Quarterly, SAGE Publication.

Maxfiled, M., & Babbie, E. (2012). *Basics of research methods* (3rd ed.). Belmont: Wadsworth.

Sadd, R., & Grinc, R. (1996). Implementation challenges in community policing: Innovative neighborhood-oriented policing in eight cities. Reprinted in *Policing Communities*.

Worrall, J. L., & Kovandzic. (2007). Cops grants and crime revisited. *Criminology, 45*, 159–190. https://doi.org/10.1111/j.1745-9125.2007.00075.x.

Zhao, J., Schneider, M., & Quint, T. (2002, November). Funding community policing to reduce crime: Have cops grants made a difference? *Criminology & Public Policy, 2*(1). ProQuest Criminal Justice.

Zhao, J., Zhang, Y., & Thurman, Q. (2011, June). Can additional resources lead to higher levels of productivity (arrests) in police agencies? *Criminal Justice Review, 36*(2), 165–182.

Chapter 3
Methodology

The Purpose of This Research

As mentioned before, studies related to community policing have established that it is valuable for both law enforcement and society to have a good relationship between the police and the community.

This relationship has been damaged by the September 11 attacks. Aggressive policing has been expanded to fight against terrorism. Some scholars agree that aggressive policing will fail (Brown 2007); others believe that community policing should be stopped in favor of the war against terrorism and "intrusive patrolling and investigative methods" (De Guzman 2002). *The gap between the two is not only a philosophical debate. These ideologies shape the policies, which dictate the direction of financial resources* (Brown 2007). Implementing the idea of curtailing community policing will be in favor of the traditional practice of policing, which consequently will allocate funds in the same direction. Some believe that community policing and Homeland Security have many things in common and can complement one another (Friedman and Cannon 2007). Therefore, to accept the provisions of Homeland Security without rejecting community policing practice, we need to adopt a new version of community policing with the approach on *Community Oriented Counter Terrorism* (Brown 2007). However, statistically speaking, it is not proven that community policing has been rejected as a major practice for agencies. One way to examine such a shift in practices is to examine the level of federal support in terms of grant allocation to community policing versus Homeland Security.

To date, there has not been a comprehensive study regarding this issue. Scholars have argued that federal funds have been reduced for community policing (De Simone 2003; Geraghty 2003) but these researches only show a snapshot of a specific time period. The entire picture must be revealed by conducting

© The Author(s), under exclusive license to Springer Nature Switzerland AG 2020
M. Alizadeh, *Police Policy Shifts After 9/11*, SpringerBriefs in Criminology,
https://doi.org/10.1007/978-3-030-32123-9_3

research to show the amount and direction of federal funds allocated to both community and Homeland Security from the date they were established. Consequently, the current research aims to examine shifts in policy that are measured by the allocation of grant-funded research. More specifically, the research will study federal funding as it pertains to community policing and Homeland Security in NYC. This process will shed light on the extension of grants on community policing prior to and after September 11 as well as examine the same process for Homeland Security. Accordingly, three specific research questions will guide this study.

Although it has been established that some negative impacts occurred during specific years that reduced the role of community policing (funds were shifted to Homeland Security instead of being allocated to community policing), whether such negative effects occurred anew each following year is not known. Do we have an example of increasing grant money for the purpose of community policing after the attacks? Or, was the money that was granted for community policing redirected to a new destination (Homeland Security) in the years following the attacks?

Research Questions

The study used a natural pre-experimental design, which is also known as the "Before-and-After Design" study. Using this design, the collected data related to the dependent variable are being compared to the data after it was exposed to an independent variable manipulation, particularly if the same group is the subject of the study before and after an independent variable is introduced to it (Gideon 2012). Using this method, the study aims to answer the following research questions:

- *How did the events of September 11 affect funding related to community policing in New York City?*
- *How did the events of September 11 affect funding related to general policing in New York City?*
- *How did the events of September 11 affect funding related to homeland security in New York City?*

There are several possible answers to these questions. One might consider examining annual budgets devoted to policing, community policing, and Homeland Security to detect any positive/negative change. Another way is to follow federal grants allocated to both community policing and Homeland Security prior to and after the September 11 attacks to learn whether funds were reduced following the attacks. The current study aims to explore these issues by examining the allocation of grant money before and after the terror attack of Sep. 11. As mentioned before, some studies show that in a particular year grant money was reduced for community policing in favor of Homeland Security. However, no research has been done documenting the entire grants' picture for Homeland Security, community policing, and general policing since 1995. To present a more comprehensive view, this research will examine these issues from three different aspects: (a) providing the total amount of grants for each year for each program since their establishments; and (b) examining the funds of community policing, general policing, and Homeland Security prior to and after the September 11 attacks in New York City.

Since one of the major September 11 attacks happened in New York City, and the attacks resulted in many policy changes at both state and federal levels, it is reasonable to assess the related policing grants on New York City.

Sample

The sample was obtained from the U.S. Census (Consolidated Federal Funds Report 2012). Using the aforementioned census, all eligible elements (all federal grants both solicited and awarded) have been examined from the unit of analysis. Hence, the researcher used the entire population (N = 29,711). As such, no sampling error is anticipated, and thus the study will have high external validity. *T-tests* and regression have been used to analyze the data.

Usually research tries to draw a sample from a larger population by developing a list that serves as an approximation of all of the cases for an entire population; this is known as a sampling frame (Kraska and Neuman 2011). However, the focus of this experiment is to examine and document any change in federal grants allocated at both the state and national levels. As such, the unit of analysis of the study is comprised of **all** federal grants awarded to community policing, general policing, and HS using federal budgets before and after September 11, 2001. The research will focus particularly on collecting related data from January 1995 to December 2010. This data will be obtained from the U.S. Census (Consolidated Federal Funds Report 2012). Using the aforementioned census, all eligible elements (all federal grants both solicited and awarded) will be examined from the unit of analysis. Hence, the researcher will use the entire population (N = 29,711). As such, no sampling error is anticipated, and thus the study will have high external validity. For example, public safety partnership and community policing grants for the year 1995 amounted to $945,838,671. In contrast, the same type of grants for the year of 1996 was $880,839,937, which is $64,998,734 less than that of the prior year. However, in 1999, the amount of community policing grants was $1,012,659,659, which is more than each of the previous years. To answer the research questions, the study aims to collect similar grants devoted to community policing for 15 years (1995–2010) as its sample. The data from 2011 to 2019 was collected from US Spending.

Data Collection

The data provided in the Consolidated Federal Funds Report (CFFR) covers federal expenditures and/or obligations for the following categories: grants, salaries, and wages, procurement contracts, direct payments for individuals, other direct payments, direct loans, guaranteed or insured loans, and insurance.

This data is in an aggregated form, which also includes all other data not related to community policing and Homeland Security. To enhance the data depth and enable further understating, the CFFR data will be supplemented by raw data available from the U.S. Census. To that extent, the researcher created a database from the U.S. Census. The researcher had reviewed grants appropriated for all programs from 1995 to 2010 (16 years) in order to extract relevant funds that were devoted to policing, community policing, and Homeland Security. The chosen data will be used to create a new set of databases for the study.

All data submitted to CFFR is assigned a program identification code, an object code, and an agency identification code. The Program Identification Code is patterned after the Catalog of Federal Domestic Assistance (CFDA). CFDA contains detailed program descriptions for **2239** federal assistance programs (CFDA 2012), which means federal grants have been awarded to 2239 different programs. Only some of them are related to the current research.

For example: Code 16.710 belongs to the Department of Justice / Office of Community Oriented Policing Services for Public Safety Partnership and Community Policing Grants. The above code remains the same for the program every single year. Therefore, the money granted under the above-mentioned code for each year has to be extracted in order to generate the database. The amount of money devoted to community policing and Homeland Security for each year has to be entered separately.

Therefore, a database has been created to supplement the information from the U.S. Census. The data related to policing, community policing, and Homeland Security of New York City has been entered separately for analysis.

For the purpose of this study CFFR codes were extracted from the Catalog of Federal Domestic Assistance. The complete CFDA has five digits, where the first two digits represent the Funding Agency and the second three digits represent the program (CFDA 2012). Using agencies listed on the website enabled the researcher to identify all codes associated with the agency. This method has been used to interpret the U.S. Census data. 29,711 Federal Assistance Programs belonging to 66 different institutions for sixteen years have been examined. Among them, the researcher identified all programs and related funds to policing, community policing, and also counter terrorism. Fifty different programs and the amount of grants they received have been identified throughout the years of 1995–2010.

Finding the related agency does not mean that all grants that have been given to them are related to community policing or Homeland Security. For instance, the Department of Homeland Security has received 101 different types of grants.

The Purpose of This Research

Table 3.1 U.S. number of grants for each year for all programs

Year	Number of grants
1995	1049
1996	990
1997	1010
1998	1030
1999	1014
2000	1027
2001	1035
2002	1059
2003	1105
2004	1131
2005	1126
2006	1135
2007	1264
2008	13,000
2009	1347
2010	1389
Total	29,711

Only some of them are related to public safety. The researcher, therefore, has to examine all of the 101 grants money by name, then categorize and narrow them down under community policing or Homeland Security. For instance, number 97.106, is a CFDA code for securing cities. Hence, it has to be classified under Homeland Security grants.

The other related issue is types of assistance. There are fourteen different types of assistance being provided by the federal government to different types of programs. Among them, two types of grants can be provided: (A) formula grants: when States or their subdivisions receive funds from the federal government by law or administrative regulation; (B) project grants: when the funds are being allocated for fixed or known periods (CFDA 2012). The current study uses formula grants for analysis, because all grants devoted to general law enforcement, community policing, or Homeland Security are being funded to the States or their components.

Table 3.1 shows the number of grants from 1995 to 2010, which were downloaded and counted for each year. The number of grants has been downloaded separately for each year to create the following chart.

Therefore, the totals of 29,711 different types of grants were reviewed in order to extract funds related to policing, community policing, and Homeland Security. After this extensive review, 52 different related grants of sixteen different years were identified and added to a separate dataset. This set of data belongs to the entire country. The process has resulted in identifying 50 related grants to policing, community policing, and Homeland Security, plus adding 2 grants related to the economy, which made for a total of 52.

The extracted information from the above-mentioned table (Table 3.1) allowed the researcher to examine only the related grants that belong to the programs that interest the current study and create new and comprehensive separate tables for NYC, which consists of the underlying data for the study. The related data is being displayed in (Table 3.2).

Intervening Variables

The research used the economy as a control variable. Macroeconomic data was used to control for three variables. Therefore, different groups of data were added to the primary data to examine whether the possible annual increase in grants is associated with deflation (GDP deflator), or overall government spending.

GDP deflator The total market value of all products and services in any given country each year is known as the Gross Domestic Product or GDP. Gross stands for total, domestic means within that country, and product is an indication of goods or services (Lups 2014). In the first adjustment, a correction was made for inflation utilizing the GDP deflator. This placed all grant dollars on a constant dollar basis, and corrects for any upward drift in grants that might occur due to inflation. GPD deflator from 1995 to 2010 was extracted from Economic Research, Federal Reserve Bank of St. Louis (2014).

U.S. Spending The third adjustment was made to account for the possibility that grants may be driven by overall government spending. Grants may increase or decrease, not due to any policy change, but simply because they are a relatively fixed percentage of a fluctuation in the government spending level. Therefore, the possible increase of funds may be due to the increase of government spending. To account for this, constant dollar grants were divided by real government spending and normalized. The relevant data for U.S. Spending was extracted from The Heritage Foundation (Frasier 2012). The final data series is the constant dollar grants as a percentage of real government spending times 10,000.

Moving Average The third adjustment utilizes a 3 year centered moving average to smooth the data and to reduce the volatility of the data. Plots of the data continue to show very high volatility from year to year, even after adjusting for government spending. Part of this volatility derives from the nature of the raw data. Each grant year data point represents new obligations provided by the federal government for that particular program. Negative numbers represent reductions in obligations for funding. This introduces greater volatility in the raw data than would likely be seen by a series that measured spending by these programs. This volatility makes it difficult to discern trends or turning points in the data. Utilization of a centered moving average maintains that time validity of the data while reducing excess variance.

Importance of Intervening Variables

Failure to address control variables in any experiment will affect the internal validity of the study. Intervening variables sometimes might be even more important than independent variables. Therefore, not isolating control variables will seriously compromise the internal validity of study (Shuttleworth 2008). The current study aims to examine the impact of 9/11 on policing grants. Hence, all other possible variables must be also measured to conclude whether or not they have any possible impact on the policing grants money. As a result, the study included all of the above mentioned intervening variables to increase the experiment's reliability.

The study aims to determine whether 9/11 was the actual independent variable in regard to increasing/decreasing of the grants, and if not, what other possible variable/s played a role, if any, in grants appropriated to community policing and Homeland Security.

Data Aggregation

Data were aggregated using the category variables. The aggregated data was used to create a table for NYC, which consists of the underlying data for the study.

New York City's Data and Data Aggregation

The obtained information from Table 3.1 was used to narrow down the data and generate a different table for NYC. The grant amounts were entered separately into different sections for each year (total of 16 years) which are displayed in Table 3.2. Since there are more than one grant for each type of policing, the total number of grants were aggregated for each category. As a result the data was classified into three sections after being associated with the control variables. The aggregated data was classified into: (a) Policing; (b) Community Policing; (c) Homeland Security.

Table 3.2 New York aggregated data and transformed data (after being associated with control variable/constant dollar/government spending)

	1995	1996	1997	1998	1999	2000	2001	2002	2003	2004	2005	2006	2007	2008	2009	2010
Policing[a]	3.8	46.9	43.5	50.3	649.8	30.2	29.2	74.2	33.4	27.1	27.7	8.2	3.6	0.0	1.2	2.2
Community policing[b]	0.0	0.0	97.3	100.5	1191.5	117.3	1.1	58.5	19.3	1.9	−0.1	2.7	−20.6	−0.1	0.0	1.4
Homeland security[c]	0.0	0.0	0.0	0.0	0.0	0.0	0.0	0.0	0.0	52.1	1.2	14.6	−8.0	68.3	185.2	10.1

[a]Policing in constant dollars / (government spending index/100)
[b]Community policing in constant dollars / (government spending index/100)
[c]Homeland Sec. in constant dollars / (government spending index/100)

Research Design and Data Analysis

The study used a natural pre-experimental design, which is also known as the "Before-and-After Design" study. Using this design, the collected data related to the dependent variable are being compared to the data after it was exposed to an independent variable manipulation, particularly if the same group is the subject of the study before and after an independent variable is introduced to it (Gideon 2012). Since the current study seeks to compare and identify trends in federal grant allocation pre- and post-September 11, such design provides an ultimate setting to calculate dollar amounts given in grants (the dependent variable in this study) before and after the mobilizing event of September 11 (the independent variable in this study). In the case of any change/s in the amount of grants after the event, one might argue that the change might have occurred because of an alternative explanation, rather than due to the September 11 attacks. The alternative explanation might be recession. If the finding shows there is a decrease in policing funds, and the reduction is due to recession, we should therefore observe the same pattern in the programs that are related to the economy. Hence, research uses economical elements (such as GDP deflator, Government spending, and grants related to the economy) as control variables. There are few grants related to the economy. Two of which are added to the data set as control variables: (A) Grants for Public Works and Economic Development Facilities; (b) Economic Development Support for Planning Organizations.

Most policy related studies use natural and quasi-experimental or pre-experimental designs since they allow an examination of a large scale of cases. Natural and quasi-experiments are different ranges of studies that have the characteristic of randomization; however, researchers have no control over assigning the randomization to the experiment. Hence researchers do *not* create natural experiments; they find them (Remler and Ryzin 2010).

As was discussed earlier, this study also discusses a large number of cases (sixteen years of the entire grants on community policing and also Homeland Security as a unit of analysis). Natural pre-experimental designs (before-and-after designs) are important for several reasons: (a) practical or ethical concerns might make the randomization impossible; (b) natural and quasi-experiment designs can be used in a bigger population, plus they have more realistic settings compared to randomized experiments, thus enabling researchers to have a much better generalization, and increasing the external validity of the results; and (c) practitioners can carry out these studies easily in their own programs (Remler and Ryzin 2010). Thus, such design is highly appropriate for policy studies such as the current one.

In natural experiments, independent variable/s of the study will occur naturally without any plan or intention to influence the outcome. Consequently, the unplanned event of 9/11 offers the unique opportunity of a natural before and after design where we can compare grant decisions before and after the occurrence of a major event. For example, Kirk (2009) examined the effects of Hurricane Katrina on residential change and the recidivism of those released from prison. Using such major events, Kirk was able to isolate the exogenous source of variation that influences recidivism to find that displacement reduces recidivism. This is very similar to the case of Sep. 11, where a major event that is exogenous has the ability to affect funding priorities and thus policy decisions.

The data that is needed to compare federal grants before and after the 9/11 event exist in the U.S. census database. By comparing the changes in funding before and after the event, the current study enables us to infer the effect of the terrorist attacks of Sep. 11 on community policing and Homeland Security funding, and thus we can also learn about how such extreme events affect national priorities and research policies to address such priorities.

Furthermore, natural experiments are known to have an acceptably high internal validity because researchers have clear evidence of cause and effect (Remler and Ryzin 2010). Thus, using such designs increases the validity of the research.

Specifically, the current study examined the history of federal grants received by both community policing and Homeland Security, and measured the grants' trends prior to and post exposure to an independent variable (September 11 attacks) by using inferential statistics, such as *T-test* and multivariate methods, (Segmented and Stepwise Regression analysis in particular) to examine the effect of independent variables (manipulation) and their interaction on the dependent variables (changes in funding).

T-test can be used when a single unit of analysis has to be studied under two different conditions (Salkind 2011). The current study aims to examine funds allocated to community policing, prior to and after September 11. Because of the fact that this study is using pre-experimental design, *T-test* is a valid statistic that is not only appropriate, but also useful to examine the funding of community policing under two different conditions (prior to and after the attack). Accordingly, independent *T-tests* are calculated before 9/11 versus after 9/11 data series. A separate *T-test* was calculated for: (1) the raw data; (2) data after inflation related variables; (3) constant dollar data as a percentage of real GDP; and (4) constant dollar data as a percentage of real government spending.

According to some researchers, the interrupted time series design is one of the strongest approaches for evaluating interventions. To make such an evaluation, Segment Regression analysis is being used as a powerful statistical tool for estimating intervention effects in interrupted time series (Wagner et al. 2002). Therefore, Segmented Regression analysis was used to try to isolate the effects of 9/11 on constant dollar grants as a percentage of real government spending. The analysis used three variables: Time (a continuous number of years since the first year of the data), Intervention (a dummy variable measuring before vs. after 9/11), and Time After (a continuous number of years after 9/11). This design attempts to estimate three parameters. The coefficient of time measures the pre-9/11 trend slope in grants. The coefficient of intervention measures the change in the level of grants immediately after 9/11. The coefficient of time after the event attempts to measure the new post 9/11-trend slope.

Therefore, the regression breaks up the data into the following components:

1. The beginning level of spending in 1995;
2. The trend line of the data between 1995 and 2019;
3. Immediate change of level right after 9/11; and
4. The difference in the trend line after 9/11

References

Brown, B. (2007). Community policing in post-September 11 America: A comment on the concept of community-oriented counterterrorism. *Police Practice and Research., 8*, 239–251.

Catalog of Federal Domestic Assistance. (2012). Extracted on 2012 May from: https://www.cfda.gov/?s=main&mode=list&tab=list&tabmode=list.

De Guzman, M. C. (2002, September-October). The changing roles and strategies of the police in a time of terror. *ACJS Today, 22*(3), 8–13.

De Simone, D. C. (2003, April). Federal budget a mixed bag for state and local governments. *Government Finance Review, 19*(2), 66–69.

Federal Reserve Bank of St. Louis, Economic research. (2014). Extracted on January 8, 2014 from: http://research.stlouisfed.org/fred2/series/GDPDEF/.

Frasier, A. A. (2012). Federal Spending by the Numbers. Special Report 121 on Budget and Spending. The Heritage Foundation. Retrieved January 8, 2014 from: http://www.heritage.org/research/reports/2012/10/federal-spending-by-the-numbers-2012.

Friedman, R., & Cannon, W. (2007). Homeland security and community policing: Competing or complementing public safety policies. *Journal of Homeland Security and Emergency Management, 4*(4).

Geraghty, J. (2003, April 9). Democratic study indicates police strain under homeland securities duties. States News Service, p. 1008099u1552.

Gideon, L. (2012). *Theories of research methodology: Readings in methods.* Dubuque: Kendall-Hunt Publishing.

Kirk, D.S. (2009). A natural experiment on residential change and recidivism: Lessons from Hurricane Katrina. *American Sociological Review, 74*(3), 484–505.

Kraska, P. B., & Neuman, W. L. (2011). *Essential criminal justice and criminology research methods.* Upper Saddle River: Pearson Education, Inc.

Lupus, J. S. (2014). Gross Domestic Product. The New Book of Knowledge. Retrieved July 24, 2014, from Grolier Online http://nbk.grolier.com.ez.lib.jjay.cuny.edu/ncpage?tn=/encyc/article.html&id=a2041781.

Remler, D., & Ryzin, G. (2010). *Research methods in practice: Strategies for description and causation* (1st ed.). Thousand Oaks: Methodology Sage Publication.

Salkind, N. (2011). *Statistics for people who hate statistics* (4th ed.). Thousand Oaks: Sage Publication.

Shuttleworth, M. (2008). *Controlled variables.* Retrieved November 08, 2014 from Explorable.com: https://explorable.com/controlled-variables.

Wagner, A. K., Soumerai, S. B., Zhang, F., & Ross-Degnan, D. (2002). Segmented regression analysis of interrupted time series studies in medication use research. *Journal of Clinical Pharmacy and Therapeutics, 27*, 299–309.

Chapter 4
Results

Plots for the graphical aggregated data, *T-tests,* and the results of regression models in the NYC policing are displayed in this part, and each section measures the allocated grant funds of all three types of policing and examines their association with intervening variables. Each section also tries to answer research questions.

NYC Community Policing Results

First research question:

How did the events of September 11 affect federal funds to community policing in New York City?

The experiment tried to answer this question in three different ways: (1) displaying aggregated raw data (2) utilizing *T-tests,* and (3) regression analysis.

1. Graphical display

The following charts displays community policing funds in the form of raw aggregated data, aggregated data controlled for inflation and government spending, and aggregated data with a 3 year moving average (Fig. 4.1).

New York community policing shows extreme variance in the community policing funds. One extremely high year makes it difficult to detect any other trends in the data. The 3 year centered moving average line takes some of the extreme volatility out of the series. It is unclear from the plot whether or not 9/11 had any impact. The main increase and decrease appears to have happened prior to 9/11. The NYC results also look reasonable because funds devoted to community policing were already down. There were not a lot of funds left to be reduced by the event. We might have seen a huge cut in funds if they were at their highest level.

© The Author(s), under exclusive license to Springer Nature Switzerland AG 2020 27
M. Alizadeh, *Police Policy Shifts After 9/11*, SpringerBriefs in Criminology,
https://doi.org/10.1007/978-3-030-32123-9_4

Fig. 4.1 NYC community policing graphical display of aggregated raw, controlled, and three-year moving average

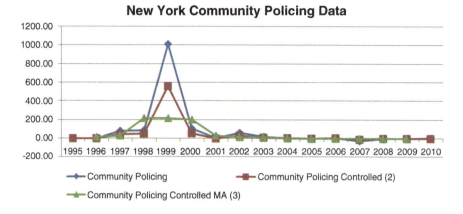

2. T-test Analysis of NYC's community policing's Funds

This section uses independent *T-test* analysis to examine the mean differences between grant funds prior to and after the terrorist attacks of 9/11, for community policing funds (Table 4.1).

The following table displays the related *T-test* data:

Table 4.1 *T-tests*, and confidence intervals of NYC community policing variables

Variables	Mean difference	T statistic	Sig
Community policing	−176.14	−1.262	0.254
Comm policing controlled[1]	−208.37	−1.27	0.251
Comm policing controlled MA[2]	−249.10	−2.75	0.040**

[1]Variables transformed to control for inflation and changes in overall government spending. Transformed variable equals untransformed variable converted to constant dollar basis by dividing by GDP deflator and then indexed to real government spending by dividing by real government spending index.
[2]3 year centered moving average of controlled variables
*One-tailed test significant at.05 level
**Significant at.05 level

T-tests Analysis of NYC Community Policing The results of the *T-test* of New York aggregated raw data for community policing appear to show a large decline in the mean from $176 million prior to 9/11 to $7 million after 9/11. This difference, however, is obscured by the very high variance of the data. Note that the *t* statistic for this difference is only −1.262, which has a p value of .254. However, the use of a three-year moving average shows a significant decline in community policing funding after 9/11 (t = −2.75, p = .040). This significant decline after the event reinforces prior evidence; and thus, further indicates that the event had a negative impact on community policing funds. Hence, less money was allocated to the community policing (Alizadeh 2015).

NYC Community Policing Results

3. Regression Analysis of NYC Community Policing Aggregated Data Controlling for Inflation, Government Spending, and a Three-Year Centered Moving Average

This section utilizes analysis of segmented regression to examine grant funds prior to and after the terrorist attacks of 9/11 for NYC's community policing's funds. The following table displays the related regression data:

Table 4.2 Regression analysis of NYC's community policing. The effect of 9/11 (independent variable) on NYC community policing grants (dependent variable)

Variable	B	T statistic	Sig
Intercept	93.56	0.543	0.599
Baseline trend variable (Year 1995 = 0 increased by 1 for each year after	35.757	0.999	0.341
Level change after 9/11event	−317.336	−1.993	0.074*
Trend change after 9/11 event	_40.457	−0950	0.365

Adjusted R2 = 0.367
F statistic = 3.510

The regression model for New York City's community policing shows a relatively moderate fit to the adjusted data. An adjusted R squared of .367 means that the model accounts for only 37% of the variance in the adjusted aggregate data. The F statistic of 3.510 is not significant at the .05 level and thus indicates that the regression equation is no better than a prediction of the mean value. None of the variables in the regression equation show significant t statistics. We have moderate evidence that 9/11 impacted community policing in New York. The regression is significant at .08 level for one variable (level change after 9/11). Although this is not strong evidence, it does suggest that there was a temporary downward effect of 9/11 on New York City's community policing funding. The mentioned trend can also be interpreted to reflect a shift in policy. We know from prior findings that community policing funds were reduced even before the event. This reduction in community policing funding was further expedited by the 9/11 events, which resulted in an even greater reduction in grants; since funds were now needed for new programs, namely Homeland Security.

Further analysis (Stepwise Regression) was used to examine the data in a greater extent. The results are displayed in the below table (Table 4.3).

Table 4.3 Stepwise regression analysis of NYC's community policing. The effect of 9/11 (independent variable) on NYC community policing grants (dependent variable)

Variable	B	T statistic	Sig
Intercept	254.465	4.341	0.001**
Trend change after 9/11 event	−249.095	−3.212	0.007**

*a stepwise regression procedure results in this variable being significant (t = −3.212, P = .007)
**significant at the .01 level

An additional analysis was also run on the NYC community policing data using a stepwise regression procedure. In this procedure, the software program automatically selects variables to be included in the regression based on their correlation with the dependent variable after controlling for all other independent variables. This procedure resulted in the intervention variable being significant (t = −3.212, p = .007). The coefficient of intervention represents the change in the level of funding from immediately before the event to immediately after the event. This provides further evidence that the level of NYC community policing funds declined immediately after the event and that the event changed funding policy.

The total results of the above analysis are displayed in the below regression line (Fig. 4.2)

Fig. 4.2 Regression line of NYC's community policing with aggregated raw data and control variables

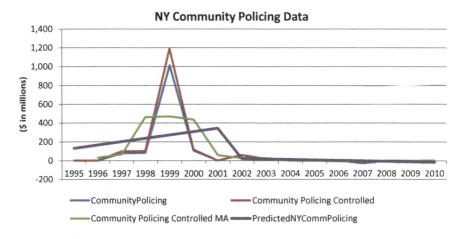

As can be seen from the regression plot, the community policing fund had its main extreme variances prior to the year 2001; however, the time intervention of 2001 shows that immediate impact of the event was to create a downward trend that might have been upward otherwise. This further supports the shift in policy because of the 9/11 attacks.

NYC General Policing Results

Second research question:

How did the events of September 11 affect federal grants of general policing in New York City?

The experiment tried to answer this question in two different ways, (1) displaying aggregated raw data (2) utilizing *T-tests,* and (3) regression analysis.

NYC General Policing Results

1. Graphical Display

The following chart displays general policing funds in the form of raw aggregated data, aggregated data controlled for inflation and government spending, and aggregated data with a 3 year moving average (Fig. 4.3).

Fig. 4.3 NYC general policing graphical display of aggregated raw, controlled, and 3 year moving average

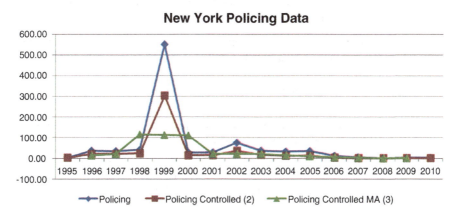

The New York data for general policing have been up and down mostly prior to the event. Funding increased in 1999 and fell back in 2000. A 3 year moving average buffers out some of this swing. However, the downward trend stayed low and never came back up after the event, due to the shift in policy.

2. *T-test* Analysis of NYC's General Policing Funds

This section uses independent T-test analysis to examine the mean differences between grant funds prior to and after the terrorist attacks of 9/11 for NYC's general policing fund. The following table displays the related T-test data:

Table 4.4 Mean differences *T-test*, and confidence intervals for New York City's policing variables

Variable	Mean difference	T statistic	Sig
Policing	−81.19	−1.076	0.322
Policing controlled[1]	−102.20	−1.154	0.292
Policing controlled MA[2]	−121.64	−2.67	0.043**

[1]Variables transformed to control for inflation and changes in overall government spending. Transformed variable equals untransformed variable converted to constant dollar basis by dividing by GDP deflator and then indexed to real government spending by dividing by real government spending index
[2]3 year centered moving average of controlled variables
**Significant at .05 level
*One-tailed test significant at .05 level

The mean funding level after 9/11 for NYC policing was $81 million lower than pre-9/11 levels, due to the extreme variance of data. This difference is not significant (t = -1.076, p = .322). Controlling for inflation and government spending also shows an insignificant change in funds.

However, using a 3 year moving average shows a significant decline in police funding after 9/11 (t = -2.67, p = .043). This decline is due to the impact of the terrorist attacks and can be translated into the policy change.

3. Regression Analysis of NYC's General Policing Aggregated Data and Controlling for Inflation, Government Spending, and a Three-Year Centered Moving Average:

This section utilizes analysis of segmented regression to examine grant funds prior to and after the terrorist attacks of 9/11 for NYC's general policing funds (Table 4.5).

The following table displays the related regression data:

Table 4.5 Regression analysis of NYC's General Policing. The effect of 9/11 (independent variable) on NYC policing grants (dependent variable)

Variable	B	T statistic	Sig
Intercept	60.754	0.708	0.495
Baseline trend variable (Year 1995 = 0 Increased by 1 for each year after)	17.996	1.009	0.337
Level change after 9/11event	−133.842	−1.687	0.122*
Trend change after 9/11 event	−25.282	−1.191	0.261

Adjusted R^2 = 0.367
F statistic= 3.511

The regression for New York general policing shows a moderate fit to the adjusted R squared of 0.367. This is an indication that the model accounts for about 37% of the variance. The F statistic of 3.511 is not significant at the .05 level. Stepwise Regression was also utilized to further examine the issue. Its analysis is displayed below:

Table 4.6 Stepwise Regression analysis of NYC's General Policing. The effect of 9/11 (independent variable) on NYC policing grants (dependent variable)

Variable	B	T statistic	Sig
Intercept	141.736	4.771	<.001**
Trend change after 9/11 event	−121.64	−3.095	0.009**

A stepwise regression procedure results in this variable being significant (t = -3.095, P = .009)
Adjusted R^2 = 0.367
F statistic= 3.511
***Significant at the .01 level*

An additional analysis was run on the NY policing data using a stepwise regression procedure, in which the software automatically selected the variables to be included in the regression based on their correlation with the dependent variable after controlling for all other independent variables. This procedure resulted in the intervention variable being significant (t = −3.095, p = .009). The coefficient of intervention represents the change in the level of funding from immediately before the event to immediately after the event. These results provide evidence that the level in NYC general policing funding declined immediately after the event and that the event changed policy. This information furnished additional proof that the catastrophic events of 9/11 reduced the funding level of policing as a result of change in policy.

The total results of the above analysis are displayed in the below regression line (Fig. 4.4)

Fig. 4.4 NYC's policing regression with aggregated raw data and control variables

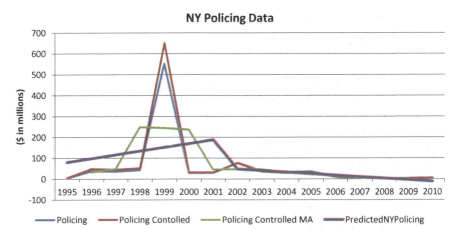

The regression plot also shows that we do have evidence to suggest that 9/11 impacted both the level and trend of funding for regular police grants in New York City.

NYC Homeland Security Results

Third research question:

How did the events of September 11 affect federal funds to homeland security in New York City?

The experiment tried to answer this question in three different ways: (1) displaying aggregated raw data (2) utilizing *T-tests*, and (3) regression analysis.

1. Graphical Display

The following charts displays Homeland Security funds in the form of raw aggregated data, aggregated data controlled for inflation, government spending, and aggregated data with a 3 year moving average (Fig. 4.5).

Fig. 4.5 NYC Homeland Security graphical display of aggregated raw and controlled data and a 3 year moving average

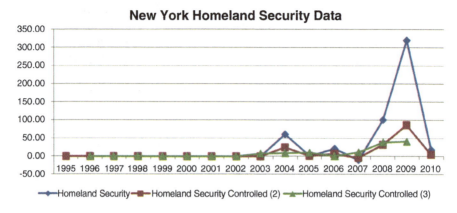

New York Homeland Security, like its U.S. counterpart, was virtually nonexistent prior to 9/11. The data show some upward trend after 9/11. The upward trend of the data after the event is a clear indication of policy change. Adding prior findings into this shows that while general and community policing funds have been declining after the event, Homeland Security funds have been increasing. This is a clear indication of a shift in the policy toward Homeland Security (Table 4.7).

2. T-test Analysis of NYC's Homeland Security's Funds

This section uses independent T-test analysis to examine the mean differences between grant funds prior to and after the terrorist attacks of 9/11, for Homeland Security's fund. The following table displays the related T-test data:

Table 4.7 Mean differences, t-tests, and confidence intervals for New York Homeland Security variables

Variable	Mean difference	T statistic	Sig
Homeland security	56.44	1.61	0.146
Homeland Sec. controlled[1]	35.75	1.75	0.119
Homeland Sec. controlled MA[2]	31.88	2.66	.032**

[1]Variables transformed to control for inflation and changes in overall government spending. Transformed variable equals untransformed variable converted to constant dollar basis by dividing by GDP deflator and then indexed to real government spending by dividing by real government spending index
[2]3 year centered moving average of controlled variables
**Significant at .05 level
*One-tailed test significant at .05 level

The table shows that when aggregated data are controlled for inflation, government spending, and a 3 year moving average, significant difference can be discerned. The data series increased from 0 prior to 9/11 to 15 after 9/11. This increase was significant as shown by the t statistic of 2.66, which has a p value of .032.

Aggregated New York Homeland Security data show an increase in mean funding from $0 prior to 9/11 to $56 million post 9/11. But due to the high variance of the data, this increase is not statistically significant. The t statistic of 1.61 has a p value of .146 and fails to be significant at the .05 level. However, using a 3 year moving average allows a significant difference to be discerned. The 3 year average data series increased from 0 prior to 9/11 to 15 after 9/11. This increase was significant as shown by the t statistic of 2.66, which has a p value of .032. These data provide further evidence that Homeland Security funds have been increasing since the years after the event, and thus an indication of policy change.

3. Regression Analysis of NYC's Homeland Security Aggregated Data Controlling for Inflation, Government Spending, and a Three-year Centered Moving Average

This section utilizes analysis of segmented regression to examine grant funds prior to and after the terrorist attacks of 9/11 for NYC's Homeland Security funds (Table 4.8).

The following table displays the related regression data:

Table 4.8 Regression analysis of NYC's Homeland security the effect of 9/11 (independent variable) on NYC Homeland grants (dependent variable)

Variable	B	T statistic	Sig
Intercept	0.0000	0.000	1
Baseline trend variable (Year 1995 = 0 Increased by 1 for each year after)	0.0000	0.000	1
Level change after 9/11event	−18.4130	−1.035	0.325
Trend change after 9/11 event	11.1770	2.347	0.041*

Adjusted R^2 = 0.684
F statistic= 10.392
*Significant at the .05 level

The regression model for New York City Homeland Security shows a moderately tight fit to the adjusted data. An adjusted R squared of .684 means that the model accounts for 68% of the variance in the adjusted aggregate data. The F statistic of 10.392 is also significant at the .002 level. Looking at the individual t statistics for the regression coefficients, we see that none of the coefficients is significant except for Time-After. The t statistic for Time-After is 2.347, which is significant at the .05 level. This means that we can reject the null hypothesis that 9/11 had no effect on the pre-existing trend in the funding of policing. Stated otherwise, we can say that we do have evidence to suggest that 9/11 positively impacted the funding trend for Homeland Security grants in New York City.

Again, this provides further evidence of the change in policy to strengthen Homeland Security by providing more funds for its programs.

The total results of the above analysis are displayed in the below regression line (Fig. 4.6)

Fig. 4.6 Plot of the aggregate data, the aggregate adjusted data, and the regression

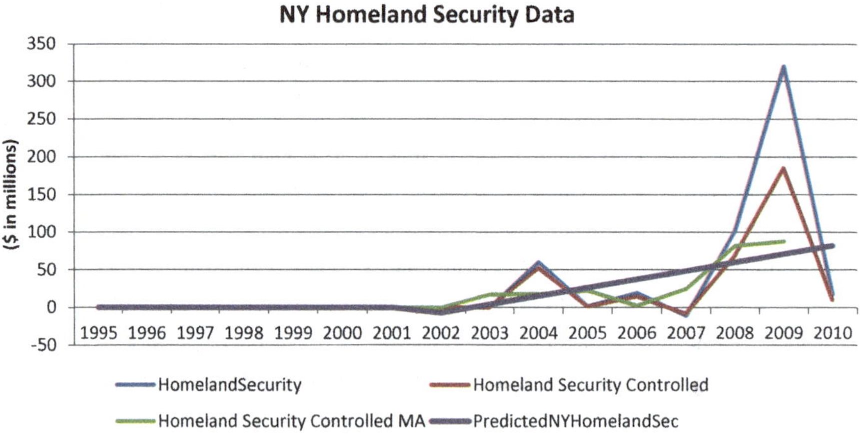

NY Homeland Security Data

New York Homeland Security, like its U.S. counterpart, was virtually nonexistent prior to 9/11. The data show some upward trend after 9/11. This has two indications: first, the programs that were not in existence before now exist; second, programs received more funds compared to general and community policing. It can be concluded that a change in policy has been made, and the new direction of policing is toward Homeland Security

NYC Policing From 2012 To 2019

Termination of the Federal Financial Statistics program resulted in termination of Consolidated Federal Fund Report (CFFR) as well. US census states:

> *"The U.S. Census Bureau has terminated the Federal Financial Statistics program effective for the FY 2012 budget. The termination of the program results in the elimination of the Consolidated Federal Funds Report (CFFR), including the publication, downloadable data, and the On-Line Query System, as well as the annual Federal Aid to States Report (FAS). In preparation for the Fiscal Year 2012 budget, the Census Bureau did a comprehensive review of a number of programs and made the difficult decision to terminate and reduce a number of existing programs in order to secure funding for new programs or cyclical increases for other programs."* (US Census 2012).

Hence, obtaining the exact similar data to follow the funds' direction is not possible. However, using the data from US Spending provided a general understanding of overall direction of the funds after 2012. The privilege of the obtained data from 1995 to 2011, was the fact that the exact amount of grants for each program made it easy to have a flawless data for analysis, while the data from US spending, do not have the details of CFFR.

Extracted data from US Spending were averaged into the Table 4.9.

Findings Summary

Table 4.9 Average of policing grants' funds from year 2011–2019

	Annual average spending 2011–2019	Percentage of annual average spending
Homeland security	9.2	92.4%
General policing	0.7	6.5%
Community policing	0.1	1.0%
Total	9.9	100%

Between 2011 and 2019 grants for Homeland Security totaled approximately $52.3 million for an average of approximately $9.2 million per year. The table was converted to the pie graph (displayed below) to visualize the data (Fig. 4.7).

Fig. 4.7 Pie graph of NYC policing from 2011–2019

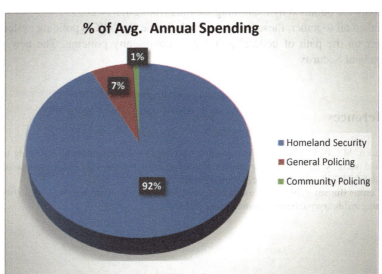

As displayed in the table and pie graph, Homeland Security spending has averaged over 90% of the total spending over the 9 year period between 2011 and 2019.

The findings are consistent with the years since 9/11, Homeland Security spending has continued to dwarf spending for General Policing (total of $2.1 million or $0.65 million per year or Community Policing (total of $.4 million or $0.1 million per year).

Findings Summary

New York City community policing data reveal an extremely high amount of funds in the year 1999. This amount decreased the year after. The *T-test* for difference in means, however, shows a significant decline in post 9/11 funding compared to pre-9/11 funding. The regression model fairly proved that NYC policing funds were reduced after the event and up to 2011. The same results were obtained by examining the data from 2012 to 2019.

New York City General Policing show the same trend as community policing. One extremely high year was followed by a sharp downward trend before the event. This fact makes it difficult to conclude the impact of the events on the funds prior to and after the event. A regression model provides more support for the existence of a downward trend in funding immediately after 9/11 as a result of a shift in policy after the 9/11 events and up to 2011. The same results were obtained by examining the data from 2012 to 2019.

New York City Homeland Security data confirm an upward trend after the events, and this trend might be considered an indication of the events' impact. Running the *T-test* after using a 3 year moving average reveals a significant level in mean prior to and after the 9/11 events. Regression also confirms a statistically significant increase in the fund trend after the 9/11 events and up to 2011. The same results were obtained by examining the data from 2012 to 2019.

Taken all together, these findings conclude that the NYC's policing system is no longer on the path of general policing or community policing. The new path is Homeland Security.

References

Alizadeh, M (2015). Shift in federal funding post Sep. 11: From community policing to homeland security (Doctoral dissertation). Retrieved from https://pdfs.semanticscholar.org/e094/adaf5974e7ff3ac869cf0e450c7137895a29.pdf.

US Census Bureau. (2012). Consolidated federal funds reports. Retrieved from https://www.census.gov/library/publications/time-series/cffr.html.

Chapter 5
Summary

Discussion

While some scholars believe the fourth model of policing (Homeland Security) has already been started (Oliver 2006), others are not sure whether Homeland Security can be considered a new model of policing. This perception is also included in some criminal justice text books (Cole et al. 2012). The shortcomings of prior research have further caused some scholars to hesitate over whether a new policing model has begun.

The uncertainty over whether the community policing era is over, has a very justifiable reason, which is a gap in the literature. Little statistical research has been available to provide a better picture as to whether a shift in policing policy occurred (Alizadeh 2015).

Using federal grants appropriated for all types of policing models, the current study aimed to examine whether policing polices have changed due to the impact of the 9/11 attacks.

As well as reviewing other literatures, the study also used theoretical background information to explore whether such an experiment was worth conducting.

The findings relate to both of the above issues (theories and other literatures).

Theoretical issues: it appears that the results of the study are consistent with the theoretical framework (based on Moral Panic and Focusing Events theories).

Study's Findings and Focusing Events Theory

A catastrophic incident will cause society to change the status quo to create better conditions that will prevent similar incidents from occurring. The focusing event can therefore be the cause of a shift in policy. If this theory is correct, we could

---

© The Author(s), under exclusive license to Springer Nature Switzerland AG 2020
M. Alizadeh, *Police Policy Shifts After 9/11*, SpringerBriefs in Criminology,
https://doi.org/10.1007/978-3-030-32123-9_5

predict that the 9/11 terrorist attacks would be considered a major focusing event. According to the theory, we should expect a major policy change after the event. The results of the study are consistent with this theory. Overall, the outcome of the experiment proves that community and general policing received fewer grant funds after the event compared to their funds before the attacks. The decrease in funds was not due to the impact of other alternative explanations (government, recession, etc.). The study examined these variables to assure that they could be excluded from the conclusions. The cause of the declining funds was not the economy. Furthermore, the study identified a different group of programs that have been receiving more grant funds while others receive less. These programs are all under the Department of Homeland Security. Subsequently, the theory appears to be correct from the current research standpoint.

The current research predominately provided solid evidence related to two different aspects of the issue. First, the *focusing event* theory appears to be correct. The research aim was not to test the focusing event theory; but inevitably, the outcome of the experiment shows the theory is reliable, at least from the current study's view. Second, the shift in the policing model did occur and the Homeland Security model shoved other policing models away, as has been discussed.

Study's Findings and Moral Panic Theory

This theory focuses on the acts of wrongdoer/s who might activate a series of events regarding an issue. They may make public demands that are exaggerated by the media to gain politicians' attention and to change policies or laws. From this view, *moral panic* can be the cause of shifts in policing policies. By reviewing the literature, one will notice that all active elements of the moral panic theory occurred after the terrorist attacks. The findings of the present study show the policy has been changed as the theory predicted. The results also show that other moderate systems (community and general policing) have been weakened.

The goal of the current research was not to test the *moral panic* theory. However, the results could not avoid showing that this theory is also correct. As was the study's aim to show, the policy change after the event became amplified. From multiple angles, the findings of the study reveal that Homeland Security prevailed over other types of policing.

Study's Findings and Other Literatures

As it was mentioned in *"Research on Funding Community Policing,"* other studies are not consistent with the outcome of the community policing model. Some studies claim that community policing grants significantly reduce both violent and property crime (Zhao et al. 2002), while others believe spending billions of dollars on community policing has little or no effect on crime reduction (Worrall and Kovandzic 2007).

Findings of the current study can help scholars on both sides to further examine their hypotheses. If community policing funds were the cause of crime reduction, we should now have more crimes, since the funds have been reduced dramatically. New opportunities are now available to test this hypothesis. The findings of the current study can be used to measure the crime rate and its possible relation to grant funds for each year. The trends of many years of community policing grant funds are now available for other researchers.

The present research also provides valuable data for those scholars who believe community policing programs funds have no impact on crime rate. If the mentioned researchers believe such programs are ineffective, they can now test the opposite version of community policing (Homeland Security) to see if its related funds lead to lower crime rates.

Providing the data for community policing grant funds was not the only objective of this research, however. The results provide a comprehensive view of grant funds for all policing model examined, which can be used for further studies.

Limitations

This experiment only reviewed federal grants. Whether the State of New York or governmental agencies are providing funds for general policing, community policing, or Homeland Security, in NYC was not the subject of this study. Future studies should address the mention issue.

The study also relies on available data. In particular, the study used the Consolidated Federal Funds Report (CFFR) and US Spending to create a database, thus assuming the data available in these reports have been collected and entered correctly by the government. Furthermore, there are two issues regarding the data:

1. The data used for the analyses were available only up to the year of 2010. Because of the financial crisis, not only has the federal government not provided related data for the years after 2010 but also the U.S. Census has stopped providing access to the entire database after the second half of 2013. Similar studies that aim to examine such data post 2011 may not be conducted due to the lack of accessibility. However, because the researcher prior to the aforementioned date downloaded the raw data from CFFR, future replication studies may rely on such data. From 2012 to 2019 the data was obtained from US Spending, which does not provide the details of CFFR.

2. Limitations of Analysis and Threats to Validity Selection: Looking at the raw data makes it clear that the composition of the aggregate data series changes across the measurement periods. Grants that were not yet inexistence in 1995 might make up a significant part of the aggregate series in 2008. This inclusion and exclusion of particular data series threatens the internal validity of the

analysis. The aggregates are composed of different items in different periods and may not be directly comparable.

Extraneous Variables It is possible but not likely that extraneous variables have a role in the policy change after 9/11. An attempt was made to control for inflation and government spending as intervening variables. However, it is possible that another factor that influences the data is at work. For example, perhaps the political party of the president makes a difference in the funding priorities as they relate to policing. We might hypothesize that certain administrations may look more favorably on a specific funding grants investigated by this study. Another potential variable that could affect funding of these types of grants is overall crime rates. Perhaps declines in funding stem from a perceived reduction in crime rates. These are possible variables that could confound our ability to attribute changes in the grant levels because of 9/11 (Alizadeh 2015).

Statistical Validity Both *T-tests* and regression analysis assume independent observations, which is clearly not the case with time series data. We need to look no further than the aggregate data for 2007 to see the role of autocorrelation in the data. The negative numbers displayed in 2007 are a clear indication that funding in previous years was excessive. Negative numbers represent a return to previously granted funds. This establishes a clear autocorrelation. The negative trend of grant funding in 2007 should be a reason to be cautious when interpreting the data.

Potential Contribution and Policy Implication

This study created a comprehensive view of grant money allocated to general policing, community policing, and Homeland Security in New York City. The researcher was able to identify trends of positive or negative changes in all three mentioned types of policing. Consequently, the shift in federal grant allocation from policing and community policing to Homeland Security is more visible, thus furthering researchers' understanding of the trends in community policing and counter terrorism. Identifying and understanding the trends in federal grant allocations will enable those who are interested in the field of policing to develop strategies to make policing programs more appealing for funding. In particular, adoption of a new version of community policing that focuses on counter terrorism is highly recommended. This recommendation will not only provide some support for the continuation of community policing strategies, but it will also address the main concerns of those who find traditional policing necessary when dealing with terrorism. Some scholars believe that many have failed to pay attention to the similarities between community policing and homeland security (Friedmann and Cannon 2007). They also believe that these two styles of policing overlap in some principles; therefore, integration of the two themes will make more sense in future research.

In order to implement this fusion, community policing funds that have been reduced or cut should be reallocated. The current study also provides useful information for other researchers to conduct further studies. For instance, now that it has been determined that community policing has been receiving less money even before the September 11 attacks, other researchers might conduct further research examining the effects of such fund reductions on crime rate.

Findings of the study indicate that general policing also has been negatively affected as a result of 9/11 events. This scenario should ring the bell even for opponents of community policing. The negative trend of general policing means fewer grants for other police tasks that are not even related to community policing. Hence, if lowering policing strength is not the best option, policy makers should act to change the current situation.

The study's results also can be used to develop policies for the Homeland Security programs as well. For instance, because of the current research, we know Homeland Security programs have been receiving more funds. Whether the extra funds have produced positive outcomes has yet to be confirmed by other research. Further research is also required to examine the militarization of police due to increasing Homeland Security's funds and to measure its impact. After all, Homeland Security has been established as a new policing model, hence, the success of its programs and policies has to be tested.

Another major contribution of the current research is the actual testing of two theories. As mentioned in the theoretical frameworks section, the current research is using the *focusing events* and *moral panic theories* to explain the conceptual background of the research.

As it was mentioned in the discussion part, negative trends in general policing after 9/11 in favor of an increase in Homeland Security funds can be explained by both of the above-mentioned theories. The outcome of the study shows that policing was negatively affected from a federal grant standpoint; therefore, the theories have been tested in the real world and shown to be valid in explaining the occurring changes.

References

Alizadeh, M (2015). Shift in federal funding post Sep. 11: From community policing to homeland security (Doctoral dissertation). Retrieved from https://pdfs.semanticscholar.org/e094/adaf5974e7ff3ac869cf0e450c7137895a29.pdf.

Cole, G., Smith, C., & DeJong, C. (2012). *The American system of criminal justice* (13th ed.). Belmont: Wadsworth Publications.

Friedmann, R., & Cannon, W. (2007). Homeland security and community policing: Competing or complementing public safety policies. *Journal of Homeland Security and Emergency Management, 4*(4).

Oliver, W. (2006). The fourth era of policing: Homeland security. *International Review of Law, Computers & Technology, 20*(1/2), 49–62. https://doi.org/10.1080/13600860600579696.

Worrall, J. L., & Kovandzic. (2007). Cops grants and crime revisited. *Criminology, 45*, 159–190. https://doi.org/10.1111/j.1745-9125.2007.00075.x.

Zhao, J., Scheider, M., & Quint, T. (2002, November). Funding community policing to reduce crime: Have cops grants made a difference? *Criminology & Public Policy, 2*(1). ProQuest Criminal Justice.

Appendix

Raw data of NYC that was extracted from 50 different grant accounts listed in Federal Census Data U.S Spending. The data in the table below represents funding for each grant for each year between 1995 and 2010. ($ are displayed in millions but full accuracy figures were used in the analysis) In addition, each grant was classified into 4 categories (1 = policing, 2 = community policing, 3 = homeland security, 4 = funding for public works and general economic purposes).

46 Appendix

Aggregated NY data

	1995	1996	1997	1998	1999	2000	2001	2002	2003	2004	2005	2006	2007	2008	2009	2010
Policing	2.85	36.60	34.73	41.43	552.28	27.10	27.14	74.61	36.09	31.14	34.32	10.88	4.89	−0.06	2.12	3.76
Community policing	0.00	0.00	77.75	82.80	1012.66	105.20	1.00	58.86	20.78	2.20	−0.06	3.55	−27.85	−0.20	0.03	2.41
Homeland security	0.00	0.00	0.00	0.00	0.00	0.00	0.00	0.00	0.03	59.84	1.50	19.29	−10.86	100.81	320.15	17.24

Control Variables

	1995	1996	1997	1998	1999	2000	2001	2002	2003	2004	2005	2006	2007	2008	2009	2010
GDP deflator	75.94	77.25	78.48	79.31	80.56	82.60	84.24	85.67	87.38	90.08	93.12	95.58	97.96	99.81	100.16	101.94
Real Gov spending	100.0	101.0	101.8	103.9	105.5	108.5	110.5	117.4	123.5	127.5	133.1	138.4	138.3	147.9	172.5	167.6

Aggregated NY data/constant dollar

	1995	1996	1997	1998	1999	2000	2001	2002	2003	2004	2005	2006	2007	2008	2009	2010
Policing	3.8	47.4	44.2	52.2	685.6	32.8	32.2	87.1	41.3	34.6	36.9	11.4	5.0	(0.1)	2.1	3.7
Community policing	–	–	99.1	104.4	1257.1	127.4	1.2	68.7	23.8	2.4	(0.1)	3.7	(28.4)	(0.2)	0.0	2.4
Homeland security	–	–	–	–	–	–	–	–	0.0	66.4	1.6	20.2	(11.1)	101.0	319.6	16.9

Aggregated NY data/constant dollar/government spending

	1995	1996	1997	1998	1999	2000	2001	2002	2003	2004	2005	2006	2007	2008	2009	2010
Policing	3.8	46.9	43.5	50.3	649.8	30.2	29.2	74.2	33.4	27.1	27.7	8.2	3.6	0.0	1.2	2.2
Community policing	0.0	0.0	97.3	100.5	1191.5	117.3	1.1	58.5	19.3	1.9	−0.1	2.7	−20.6	−0.1	0.0	1.4
Homeland security	0.0	0.0	0.0	0.0	0.0	0.0	0.0	0.0	0.0	52.1	1.2	14.6	−8.0	68.3	185.2	10.1

Index

A
Annual budgets, 16
Antiterrorism Act, 12
Aviation Security Improvement Act, 3

B
Before-and-After Design study, 16, 23

C
Catalog of Federal Domestic Assistance
(CFDA), 18
Community Oriented Counter Terrorism, 15
Community Oriented Policing Services
(COPS), 1, 2, 9–11
Community policing (CP)
claimed, 1
Community Oriented Counter Terrorism, 15
complimentary strategies, 8
concept, 7
funding, 9, 10
grants trend (*see* Grants trend in CP)
and HS (*see* Homeland Security (HS))
implementation, 10, 11
Likert scale, 7
national surveys, 7–9
negative impacts, 16
ORC, 7
organizational policies, 1
PERF, 7
police agencies, 8
practice, 8, 14
requirement, 12

September 11, 11–13
surveys, 7, 8
Consolidated Federal Funds Reports (CFFR),
36, 41
aggressive policing, 15
allocation of grant money, 16
Before-and-After Design study, 16
data collection, 18–20, 22
grants, 19
intervening variables, 20–21
intrusive patrolling and investigative
methods, 15
research design and data analysis, 23–25
research questions, 16
samples, 17
time period, 15
types of assistance, 19
Contribution, 42, 43
Control variables, 46
CP funding, 9, 10
CP National Survey, 8, 9
Cross-sectional studies, 13

D
Data aggregation, 21
Direct loans, 18
Direct payments for individuals, 18

E
Economical elements, 23
Extend of CP, 7, 13
Extraneous variables, 42

© The Author(s), under exclusive license to Springer Nature Switzerland AG 2020
M. Alizadeh, *Police Policy Shifts After 9/11*, SpringerBriefs in Criminology,
https://doi.org/10.1007/978-3-030-32123-9

Index

F

Focusing events theory, 39, 40
  aviation policy modification, 3
  changing and shifting governments'
     funding, 3
  explosion of TWA flight 800, 3
  hijacking of planes, 3
  Pan Am flight 103 bombing over
     Lockerbie, 3
  safety review, 3
  scholars, 2
  September 11, 4, 5
  society's reaction, 2
  stress tests, 3
Folk devils, 4, 5

G

GDP deflator, 20
Grant-funded research, 16
Grant money, 16
Grants, 18, 19
Grants trend in CP, 37
  graphical display
    aggregated data controlled, 27, 28
    funds, 27
    raw aggregated data, 27, 28
  regression analysis, 29
  regression line, 30
  September 11, 27
  stepwise regression, 29, 30
  t-tests analysis, 28
Grants trend in general policing, 38
  aggregated raw data and control variables,
    33
  graphical display, 31
  regression analysis, 32
  stepwise regression, 32
  t-test analysis, 31, 32
Grants trend in HS, 38
  graphical display, 33, 34
  regression analysis, 35, 36
  t-test analysis, 34, 35
Guaranteed/insured loans, 18

H

Hijackers, 5
Homeland Security (HS)
  complimentary strategies, 8
  and CP (*see* Community policing (CP))
  criminal justice text books, 39
  department, 3
  establishment, 2

  goals, 3, 12
  grants trend (*see* Grants trend in HS)
  influence, 2
  Pentagon, 12
  police agencies, 12
  unprecedented level, 2
  U.S.A. PATRIOT Act, 12, 13
  World Trade Center, 12

I

Implementation, CP, 10, 11
Innovative Neighborhood Oriented Policing
    (INOP) programs, 10, 11
Insurance, 18
Intelligence gatherers, 2
Internal validity, 21
Intervening variables
  GDP deflator, 20
  independent variable, 21
  macroeconomic data, 20
  moving average, 20, 21
  U.S. Spending, 20
Intrusive patrolling and investigative methods,
    15

L

Law enforcement, 15
Likert scale, 7
Limitations
  CFFR, 41
  contribution, 42–43
  data, 41
  extraneous variables, 42
  governmental agencies, 41
  policy implication, 42–43
  selection, 41
  statistical validity, 42

M

Macroeconomic data, 20
Making Hiring Officer Redeployment
    Effective (MORE) funds, 1
Moral panic theory, 40
  Ben-Yehuda and Goode, 5
  communities' reactions, 4
  elements, 4
  folk devils, 4
  in Los Angeles, 4
  September 11, 5
  sexual psychopaths, 4
  variety of actors, 4

Index

N
Natural and quasi-experiments, 23
Natural experiments, 23, 24
Natural pre-experimental designs, 23
New York City (NYC)
    data and data aggregation, 21
    data/constant dollar, 46
    government spending, 46
    Policing Policy, 1
    raw data, 45
NYC Policing from 2012 to 2019, 36, 37

O
Opinion Research Corporation Company
    (ORC), 7
Organizational policies, 1

P
Police Executive Research Forum (PERF), 7,
    8, 11
Police Foundation, 7
Police policy
    COPS, 1, 2
    focusing events (*see* Focusing events
        theory)
    moral panic (*see* Moral panic theory)
    pre-experimental design, 1
    shift in, 1
Policy implication, 42, 43
Policy recommendations, 42
Pre-experimental design, 13
Procurement contracts, 18
Program Identification Code, 18

R
Research on Funding Community Policing,
    40, 41

S
Salaries, 18
Sampling frame, 17
Segment Regression analysis, 24
Sexual psychopaths, 4, 5
Shift in police policy, 1
Society, 15
Statistical validity, 42
Stepwise regression, 29, 30, 32

T
Theoretical issues, 39
T-test, 24
    CP (*see* Grants trend in CP)
    general policing (*see* Grants trend in
        general policing)
    HS (*see* Grants trend in HS)

U
U.S.A. PATRIOT Act, 12, 13

V
Violent Crime Control Act, 1

W
Wages, 18

9783030321222